50 Satisfying Vegetarian BBQ Recipes

By: Kelly Johnson

Table of Contents

- Grilled Vegetable Skewers
- BBQ Portobello Mushroom Burgers
- Grilled Corn on the Cob with Herb Butter
- Smoky Eggplant Dip
- Spicy Grilled Tofu Steaks
- BBQ Cauliflower Bites
- Grilled Stuffed Peppers
- Vegetable Kebabs with Chimichurri
- BBQ Lentil Sliders
- Grilled Pineapple with Coconut Rum Glaze
- Zucchini Noodles with Grilled Vegetables
- BBQ Chickpea Salad
- Grilled Caprese Salad Skewers
- BBQ Jackfruit Sandwiches
- Grilled Asparagus with Lemon Zest
- Smoky Black Bean Tacos
- Grilled Sweet Potatoes with Maple Glaze
- Spicy Grilled Tempeh
- Grilled Ratatouille
- BBQ Beetroot Burgers
- Grilled Peach and Arugula Salad
- BBQ Mushroom Quesadillas
- Grilled Eggplant with Tahini Sauce
- BBQ Vegetable Pizza
- Grilled Avocado with Lime Dressing
- BBQ Chickpea Burger
- Grilled Carrots with Cumin and Honey
- Mediterranean Grilled Vegetable Platter
- Grilled Quinoa-Stuffed Bell Peppers
- BBQ Cauliflower Steaks
- Spicy Grilled Corn Salad
- Grilled Spinach and Feta Stuffed Portobellos
- BBQ Sweet Potato Wedges
- Grilled Vegetable Fajitas
- BBQ Vegetable Flatbreads

- Grilled Garlic and Herb Zucchini
- BBQ Lentil and Quinoa Salad
- Grilled Watermelon Salad
- BBQ Mushroom and Black Bean Chili
- Grilled Stuffed Zucchini Boats
- Smoky BBQ Pasta Salad
- Grilled Pita with Hummus and Vegetables
- BBQ Roasted Brussels Sprouts
- Grilled Radishes with Butter
- BBQ Jerk Tofu
- Grilled Tomato and Mozzarella Salad
- BBQ Vegetable Stir-Fry
- Grilled Citrus Marinated Tofu
- BBQ Chickpea and Avocado Wraps
- Grilled Fruit Skewers

Grilled Vegetable Skewers

Ingredients:

- 1 zucchini, sliced
- 1 bell pepper (any color), chopped
- 1 red onion, cut into chunks
- 1 cup cherry tomatoes
- 1 cup mushrooms, whole
- ¼ cup olive oil
- 2 cloves garlic, minced
- Salt and pepper to taste
- Skewers (soaked in water if wooden)

Instructions:

1. **Prepare Skewers:** Thread the vegetables onto the skewers, alternating types for variety.
2. **Make Marinade:** In a bowl, whisk together olive oil, minced garlic, salt, and pepper.
3. **Marinate Vegetables:** Brush the skewers with the marinade and let them sit for 15-30 minutes.
4. **Preheat Grill:** Preheat the grill to medium-high heat.
5. **Grill Skewers:** Place the skewers on the grill and cook for about 10-15 minutes, turning occasionally until the vegetables are tender and slightly charred.
6. **Serve:** Remove from the grill and serve warm.

BBQ Portobello Mushroom Burgers

Ingredients:

- 4 large portobello mushrooms, stems removed
- ¼ cup balsamic vinegar
- 2 tbsp olive oil
- 2 cloves garlic, minced
- ½ tsp salt
- ½ tsp black pepper
- 4 burger buns
- Lettuce, tomato, and your choice of condiments

Instructions:

1. **Marinate Mushrooms:** In a bowl, combine balsamic vinegar, olive oil, minced garlic, salt, and pepper. Add the mushrooms and marinate for at least 30 minutes.
2. **Preheat Grill:** Preheat the grill to medium heat.
3. **Grill Mushrooms:** Place the mushrooms on the grill, gill side down, and cook for 5-7 minutes. Flip and cook for another 5-7 minutes until tender.
4. **Assemble Burgers:** Toast the burger buns on the grill. Place a grilled mushroom on each bun and top with lettuce, tomato, and your favorite condiments.
5. **Serve:** Serve immediately.

Grilled Corn on the Cob with Herb Butter

Ingredients:

- 4 ears of corn, husked
- ½ cup unsalted butter, softened
- 2 tbsp fresh parsley, chopped
- 1 tbsp fresh chives, chopped
- 1 tsp garlic powder
- Salt and pepper to taste

Instructions:

1. **Make Herb Butter:** In a bowl, mix the softened butter, parsley, chives, garlic powder, salt, and pepper until well combined.
2. **Preheat Grill:** Preheat the grill to medium heat.
3. **Grill Corn:** Place the corn directly on the grill and cook for about 10-15 minutes, turning occasionally until charred and tender.
4. **Add Butter:** Remove the corn from the grill and brush with the herb butter while still hot.
5. **Serve:** Serve warm.

Smoky Eggplant Dip

Ingredients:

- 1 large eggplant
- 2 tbsp olive oil
- 2 cloves garlic, minced
- 2 tbsp tahini
- 2 tbsp lemon juice
- ½ tsp smoked paprika
- Salt and pepper to taste

Instructions:

1. **Preheat Grill:** Preheat the grill to medium-high heat.
2. **Grill Eggplant:** Cut the eggplant in half lengthwise and brush the cut sides with olive oil. Grill for about 10-15 minutes, cut side down, until soft and smoky.
3. **Make Dip:** In a food processor, combine the grilled eggplant, garlic, tahini, lemon juice, smoked paprika, salt, and pepper. Blend until smooth.
4. **Serve:** Transfer to a bowl and serve with pita chips or fresh vegetables.

Spicy Grilled Tofu Steaks

Ingredients:

- 1 block firm tofu, pressed and sliced into steaks
- ¼ cup soy sauce
- 2 tbsp sriracha
- 1 tbsp maple syrup
- 1 tbsp olive oil
- 1 tsp garlic powder
- Salt and pepper to taste

Instructions:

1. **Marinate Tofu:** In a bowl, mix soy sauce, sriracha, maple syrup, olive oil, garlic powder, salt, and pepper. Add the tofu steaks and marinate for at least 30 minutes.
2. **Preheat Grill:** Preheat the grill to medium heat.
3. **Grill Tofu:** Place the marinated tofu on the grill and cook for about 5-7 minutes on each side, until grill marks appear and the tofu is heated through.
4. **Serve:** Serve hot with a side of grilled vegetables or salad.

BBQ Cauliflower Bites

Ingredients:

- 1 head of cauliflower, cut into bite-sized florets
- ½ cup BBQ sauce
- 2 tbsp olive oil
- Salt and pepper to taste

Instructions:

1. **Preheat Grill:** Preheat the grill to medium heat.
2. **Prepare Cauliflower:** In a bowl, toss the cauliflower florets with olive oil, salt, and pepper.
3. **Grill Cauliflower:** Place the cauliflower in a grill basket and grill for about 10-15 minutes, stirring occasionally until tender and charred.
4. **Add BBQ Sauce:** In the last few minutes of cooking, drizzle BBQ sauce over the cauliflower and toss to coat. Grill for an additional 2-3 minutes.
5. **Serve:** Serve warm as a side dish or appetizer.

Grilled Stuffed Peppers

Ingredients:

- 4 bell peppers, halved and seeds removed
- 1 cup cooked rice (or quinoa)
- 1 cup black beans, drained and rinsed
- 1 cup corn
- 1 cup salsa
- 1 tsp cumin
- 1 cup shredded cheese (optional)

Instructions:

1. **Preheat Grill:** Preheat the grill to medium heat.
2. **Prepare Filling:** In a bowl, mix cooked rice, black beans, corn, salsa, and cumin.
3. **Stuff Peppers:** Fill each pepper half with the rice mixture and top with shredded cheese if using.
4. **Grill Peppers:** Wrap the stuffed peppers in foil and grill for 15-20 minutes until the peppers are tender.
5. **Serve:** Remove from the grill and serve warm.

Vegetable Kebabs with Chimichurri

Ingredients:

- 1 zucchini, sliced
- 1 bell pepper, chopped
- 1 red onion, cut into chunks
- 1 cup cherry tomatoes
- ¼ cup olive oil
- Salt and pepper to taste
- Skewers (soaked in water if wooden)
- **For Chimichurri:**
    - ½ cup fresh parsley, chopped
    - ¼ cup olive oil
    - 2 tbsp red wine vinegar
    - 2 cloves garlic, minced
    - ½ tsp red pepper flakes
    - Salt and pepper to taste

Instructions:

1. **Prepare Skewers:** Thread the vegetables onto the skewers, alternating types.
2. **Make Chimichurri:** In a bowl, combine parsley, olive oil, red wine vinegar, garlic, red pepper flakes, salt, and pepper.
3. **Marinate Skewers:** Brush the skewers with olive oil and season with salt and pepper. Let them sit for about 15 minutes.
4. **Preheat Grill:** Preheat the grill to medium-high heat.
5. **Grill Skewers:** Grill the vegetable skewers for about 10-15 minutes, turning occasionally until charred and tender.
6. **Serve:** Drizzle with chimichurri before serving. Enjoy!

BBQ Lentil Sliders

Ingredients:

- 1 cup cooked lentils
- ½ cup breadcrumbs
- ¼ cup finely chopped onion
- ¼ cup grated carrot
- 2 cloves garlic, minced
- 1 tbsp BBQ sauce
- 1 tsp smoked paprika
- Salt and pepper to taste
- Slider buns
- Optional toppings: lettuce, tomato, pickles

Instructions:

1. **Prepare Mixture:** In a bowl, mash the lentils slightly and mix in breadcrumbs, onion, carrot, garlic, BBQ sauce, smoked paprika, salt, and pepper until combined.
2. **Form Patties:** Shape the mixture into small patties.
3. **Preheat Grill:** Preheat the grill to medium heat.
4. **Grill Sliders:** Cook the patties on the grill for about 5-7 minutes on each side until heated through and slightly crispy.
5. **Assemble Sliders:** Place the patties on slider buns and add your choice of toppings. Serve warm.

Grilled Pineapple with Coconut Rum Glaze

Ingredients:

- 1 ripe pineapple, peeled and sliced into rings
- ¼ cup coconut rum
- 2 tbsp brown sugar
- 1 tbsp lime juice
- 1 tbsp melted coconut oil

Instructions:

1. **Make Glaze:** In a bowl, whisk together coconut rum, brown sugar, lime juice, and melted coconut oil.
2. **Preheat Grill:** Preheat the grill to medium-high heat.
3. **Grill Pineapple:** Brush the pineapple slices with the glaze and place them on the grill. Cook for about 3-4 minutes on each side until caramelized and grill marks appear.
4. **Serve:** Remove from the grill and drizzle with any remaining glaze. Enjoy warm or at room temperature.

Zucchini Noodles with Grilled Vegetables

Ingredients:

- 2 medium zucchinis, spiralized
- 1 bell pepper, sliced
- 1 red onion, sliced
- 1 cup cherry tomatoes, halved
- 2 tbsp olive oil
- Salt and pepper to taste
- 1 tsp Italian seasoning
- Grated Parmesan cheese (optional)

Instructions:

1. **Preheat Grill:** Preheat the grill to medium heat.
2. **Grill Vegetables:** Toss the bell pepper, onion, and tomatoes with olive oil, salt, pepper, and Italian seasoning. Grill the vegetables for about 5-7 minutes until tender.
3. **Cook Zucchini Noodles:** In a separate pan, lightly sauté the zucchini noodles for 2-3 minutes until just tender.
4. **Combine:** Toss the grilled vegetables with the zucchini noodles.
5. **Serve:** Top with grated Parmesan cheese if desired. Serve warm.

BBQ Chickpea Salad

Ingredients:

- 1 can chickpeas, drained and rinsed
- 1 bell pepper, chopped
- 1 cup corn (canned or frozen)
- ¼ cup red onion, diced
- ¼ cup BBQ sauce
- 2 tbsp olive oil
- Salt and pepper to taste
- Optional toppings: avocado, cilantro

Instructions:

1. **Combine Ingredients:** In a bowl, mix chickpeas, bell pepper, corn, and red onion.
2. **Dress Salad:** Drizzle with BBQ sauce and olive oil, then season with salt and pepper. Toss to combine.
3. **Serve:** Serve chilled or at room temperature, topped with avocado and cilantro if desired.

Grilled Caprese Salad Skewers

Ingredients:

- 1 cup cherry tomatoes
- 1 cup fresh mozzarella balls
- Fresh basil leaves
- 2 tbsp balsamic glaze
- Salt and pepper to taste
- Skewers

Instructions:

1. **Assemble Skewers:** On each skewer, thread a cherry tomato, a basil leaf, and a mozzarella ball. Repeat until the skewer is filled.
2. **Preheat Grill:** Preheat the grill to medium heat.
3. **Grill Skewers:** Grill the skewers for about 2-3 minutes on each side until the tomatoes are slightly blistered.
4. **Serve:** Drizzle with balsamic glaze and sprinkle with salt and pepper. Serve warm.

BBQ Jackfruit Sandwiches

Ingredients:

- 1 can young green jackfruit in brine, drained and rinsed
- ½ cup BBQ sauce
- 1 tbsp olive oil
- ½ cup onion, chopped
- Slider or burger buns
- Optional toppings: coleslaw

Instructions:

1. **Prepare Jackfruit:** In a pan, heat olive oil over medium heat and sauté onion until translucent. Add jackfruit and cook for about 5-7 minutes, breaking it apart with a fork.
2. **Add BBQ Sauce:** Stir in BBQ sauce and cook for another 5-10 minutes until heated through and well-coated.
3. **Preheat Grill:** Preheat the grill to medium heat.
4. **Assemble Sandwiches:** Serve the BBQ jackfruit on buns, topped with coleslaw if desired.

Grilled Asparagus with Lemon Zest

Ingredients:

- 1 lb asparagus, trimmed
- 2 tbsp olive oil
- Zest of 1 lemon
- Salt and pepper to taste

Instructions:

1. **Preheat Grill:** Preheat the grill to medium-high heat.
2. **Prepare Asparagus:** Toss asparagus with olive oil, lemon zest, salt, and pepper.
3. **Grill Asparagus:** Place asparagus directly on the grill or use a grill basket. Grill for about 5-7 minutes, turning occasionally, until tender.
4. **Serve:** Serve warm as a side dish.

Smoky Black Bean Tacos

Ingredients:

- 1 can black beans, drained and rinsed
- 1 tsp smoked paprika
- ½ tsp cumin
- Salt and pepper to taste
- Corn tortillas
- Optional toppings: avocado, salsa, cilantro

Instructions:

1. **Prepare Filling:** In a pan, combine black beans, smoked paprika, cumin, salt, and pepper. Heat over medium heat until warmed through.
2. **Preheat Grill:** Preheat the grill to medium heat.
3. **Grill Tortillas:** Grill corn tortillas for about 1 minute on each side until warmed and slightly charred.
4. **Assemble Tacos:** Fill each tortilla with the black bean mixture and top with avocado, salsa, and cilantro as desired. Serve immediately.

Grilled Sweet Potatoes with Maple Glaze

Ingredients:

- 2 medium sweet potatoes, peeled and sliced into rounds
- 3 tbsp olive oil
- 3 tbsp maple syrup
- 1 tsp cinnamon
- Salt and pepper to taste
- Chopped fresh parsley for garnish

Instructions:

1. **Prepare Sweet Potatoes:** In a bowl, combine olive oil, maple syrup, cinnamon, salt, and pepper. Add the sweet potato slices and toss to coat.
2. **Preheat Grill:** Preheat the grill to medium heat.
3. **Grill Sweet Potatoes:** Place the sweet potato slices on the grill. Cook for about 4-5 minutes on each side until tender and grill marks appear.
4. **Serve:** Remove from the grill, garnish with chopped parsley, and serve warm.

Spicy Grilled Tempeh

Ingredients:

- 1 block (8 oz) tempeh, sliced into thin strips
- 3 tbsp soy sauce
- 1 tbsp sriracha (adjust to taste)
- 1 tbsp maple syrup
- 2 cloves garlic, minced
- 1 tbsp olive oil

Instructions:

1. **Marinate Tempeh:** In a bowl, mix soy sauce, sriracha, maple syrup, minced garlic, and olive oil. Add the tempeh strips and marinate for at least 30 minutes.
2. **Preheat Grill:** Preheat the grill to medium-high heat.
3. **Grill Tempeh:** Place the tempeh on the grill and cook for about 4-5 minutes on each side until crispy and charred.
4. **Serve:** Serve warm as a protein-packed addition to salads or sandwiches.

Grilled Ratatouille

Ingredients:

- 1 zucchini, sliced
- 1 eggplant, sliced
- 1 bell pepper, sliced
- 1 onion, sliced
- 2 tbsp olive oil
- 1 tsp dried thyme
- Salt and pepper to taste
- Fresh basil for garnish

Instructions:

1. **Prepare Vegetables:** In a bowl, toss the sliced vegetables with olive oil, thyme, salt, and pepper.
2. **Preheat Grill:** Preheat the grill to medium heat.
3. **Grill Vegetables:** Place the vegetables directly on the grill or in a grill basket. Grill for about 5-7 minutes, turning occasionally until tender and slightly charred.
4. **Serve:** Garnish with fresh basil and serve warm.

BBQ Beetroot Burgers

Ingredients:

- 2 cups cooked beetroot, finely chopped
- 1 cup cooked black beans, mashed
- 1/2 cup breadcrumbs
- 1/4 cup red onion, finely chopped
- 2 cloves garlic, minced
- 1 tsp cumin
- Salt and pepper to taste
- Olive oil for grilling

Instructions:

1. **Mix Ingredients:** In a bowl, combine the beetroot, black beans, breadcrumbs, red onion, garlic, cumin, salt, and pepper. Mix until well combined.
2. **Form Patties:** Shape the mixture into burger patties.
3. **Preheat Grill:** Preheat the grill to medium heat. Brush the grill with olive oil.
4. **Grill Patties:** Grill the patties for about 5-6 minutes on each side until heated through and slightly crispy.
5. **Serve:** Serve on buns with your favorite toppings.

Grilled Peach and Arugula Salad

Ingredients:

- 2 ripe peaches, halved and pitted
- 4 cups arugula
- 1/4 cup feta cheese, crumbled
- 1/4 cup walnuts, toasted
- 2 tbsp olive oil
- 1 tbsp balsamic vinegar
- Salt and pepper to taste

Instructions:

1. **Preheat Grill:** Preheat the grill to medium heat.
2. **Grill Peaches:** Brush the cut sides of the peaches with olive oil and grill for 2-3 minutes until grill marks appear.
3. **Prepare Salad:** In a bowl, combine arugula, feta cheese, and walnuts.
4. **Dress Salad:** Drizzle with olive oil, balsamic vinegar, salt, and pepper. Toss to combine.
5. **Serve:** Top the salad with grilled peaches and serve immediately.

BBQ Mushroom Quesadillas

Ingredients:

- 2 cups mushrooms, sliced
- 1 cup shredded cheese (cheddar or mozzarella)
- 4 large tortillas
- 2 tbsp BBQ sauce
- 1 tbsp olive oil
- Fresh cilantro for garnish

Instructions:

1. **Sauté Mushrooms:** In a skillet, heat olive oil over medium heat. Add mushrooms and sauté until browned, about 5-7 minutes.
2. **Assemble Quesadillas:** Spread BBQ sauce on one half of each tortilla. Top with sautéed mushrooms and cheese. Fold the tortillas in half.
3. **Grill Quesadillas:** Preheat the grill to medium heat. Grill the quesadillas for about 3-4 minutes on each side until golden brown and the cheese is melted.
4. **Serve:** Cut into wedges and garnish with fresh cilantro.

Grilled Eggplant with Tahini Sauce

Ingredients:

- 1 large eggplant, sliced into rounds
- 3 tbsp olive oil
- Salt and pepper to taste
- 1/4 cup tahini
- 2 tbsp lemon juice
- 1 clove garlic, minced
- Water to thin (if needed)

Instructions:

1. **Prepare Eggplant:** Brush the eggplant slices with olive oil and season with salt and pepper.
2. **Preheat Grill:** Preheat the grill to medium heat.
3. **Grill Eggplant:** Grill the eggplant slices for about 4-5 minutes on each side until tender and grill marks appear.
4. **Make Tahini Sauce:** In a bowl, mix tahini, lemon juice, minced garlic, salt, and enough water to reach your desired consistency.
5. **Serve:** Drizzle the tahini sauce over the grilled eggplant and serve warm.

BBQ Vegetable Pizza

Ingredients:

- 1 pre-made pizza crust
- 1/2 cup BBQ sauce
- 1 cup bell peppers, sliced
- 1 cup red onion, sliced
- 1 cup zucchini, sliced
- 1 cup shredded mozzarella cheese
- Fresh basil for garnish

Instructions:

1. **Preheat Grill:** Preheat the grill to medium heat.
2. **Prepare Vegetables:** Toss bell peppers, onion, and zucchini with a little olive oil and season with salt and pepper.
3. **Assemble Pizza:** Spread BBQ sauce over the pizza crust. Top with grilled vegetables and sprinkle with mozzarella cheese.
4. **Grill Pizza:** Place the pizza on the grill and cover. Grill for about 8-10 minutes until the cheese is melted and the crust is crispy.
5. **Serve:** Remove from the grill, garnish with fresh basil, and slice to serve.

Enjoy your delicious grilled and BBQ dishes!

Grilled Avocado with Lime Dressing

Ingredients:

- 2 ripe avocados, halved and pitted
- 2 tbsp olive oil
- 1 lime, juiced
- Salt and pepper to taste
- Fresh cilantro for garnish

Instructions:

1. **Preheat Grill:** Preheat the grill to medium heat.
2. **Prepare Avocados:** Brush the cut sides of the avocados with olive oil and season with salt and pepper.
3. **Grill Avocados:** Place the avocados cut side down on the grill. Grill for about 3-4 minutes until grill marks appear.
4. **Make Dressing:** In a small bowl, mix lime juice, olive oil, salt, and pepper.
5. **Serve:** Drizzle the dressing over the grilled avocados and garnish with fresh cilantro.

BBQ Chickpea Burger

Ingredients:

- 1 can (15 oz) chickpeas, drained and rinsed
- 1/2 cup breadcrumbs
- 1/4 cup onion, finely chopped
- 2 cloves garlic, minced
- 2 tbsp BBQ sauce
- 1 tsp smoked paprika
- Salt and pepper to taste
- Olive oil for grilling

Instructions:

1. **Mix Ingredients:** In a bowl, mash the chickpeas with a fork. Add breadcrumbs, onion, garlic, BBQ sauce, smoked paprika, salt, and pepper. Mix well.
2. **Form Patties:** Shape the mixture into burger patties.
3. **Preheat Grill:** Preheat the grill to medium heat. Brush the grill with olive oil.
4. **Grill Patties:** Grill the patties for about 5-6 minutes on each side until heated through and crispy.
5. **Serve:** Serve on buns with your favorite toppings.

Grilled Carrots with Cumin and Honey

Ingredients:

- 4 large carrots, peeled and cut into sticks
- 2 tbsp olive oil
- 1 tbsp honey
- 1 tsp ground cumin
- Salt and pepper to taste

Instructions:

1. **Prepare Carrots:** In a bowl, mix olive oil, honey, cumin, salt, and pepper. Toss the carrot sticks in the mixture to coat.
2. **Preheat Grill:** Preheat the grill to medium heat.
3. **Grill Carrots:** Grill the carrots for about 10-12 minutes, turning occasionally until tender and caramelized.
4. **Serve:** Remove from the grill and serve warm.

Mediterranean Grilled Vegetable Platter

Ingredients:

- 1 zucchini, sliced
- 1 eggplant, sliced
- 1 bell pepper, sliced
- 1 red onion, sliced
- 1/4 cup olive oil
- 2 tsp Italian seasoning
- Salt and pepper to taste

Instructions:

1. **Prepare Vegetables:** In a bowl, toss the vegetables with olive oil, Italian seasoning, salt, and pepper.
2. **Preheat Grill:** Preheat the grill to medium heat.
3. **Grill Vegetables:** Place the vegetables directly on the grill or in a grill basket. Grill for about 8-10 minutes, turning occasionally until tender.
4. **Serve:** Arrange the grilled vegetables on a platter and serve warm.

Grilled Quinoa-Stuffed Bell Peppers

Ingredients:

- 4 bell peppers, halved and seeds removed
- 1 cup cooked quinoa
- 1 cup black beans, drained and rinsed
- 1/2 cup corn (fresh or frozen)
- 1 tsp cumin
- 1/2 cup shredded cheese (optional)

Instructions:

1. **Preheat Grill:** Preheat the grill to medium heat.
2. **Mix Filling:** In a bowl, combine cooked quinoa, black beans, corn, cumin, and salt and pepper to taste.
3. **Stuff Peppers:** Fill each bell pepper half with the quinoa mixture.
4. **Grill Peppers:** Place the stuffed peppers on the grill. Cover and cook for about 10-15 minutes until the peppers are tender. If using cheese, sprinkle it on top during the last 5 minutes of cooking.
5. **Serve:** Serve warm as a delicious and nutritious dish.

BBQ Cauliflower Steaks

Ingredients:

- 1 large head of cauliflower, cut into 1-inch thick steaks
- 1/4 cup BBQ sauce
- 2 tbsp olive oil
- Salt and pepper to taste

Instructions:

1. **Preheat Grill:** Preheat the grill to medium heat.
2. **Prepare Cauliflower:** Brush both sides of the cauliflower steaks with olive oil and season with salt and pepper.
3. **Grill Cauliflower:** Place the cauliflower steaks on the grill and cook for about 5-7 minutes on each side, brushing with BBQ sauce during the last few minutes.
4. **Serve:** Serve warm as a hearty side dish or main course.

Spicy Grilled Corn Salad

Ingredients:

- 4 ears of corn, husked
- 1 red bell pepper, diced
- 1/4 cup red onion, diced
- 1 jalapeño, minced
- 2 tbsp lime juice
- 2 tbsp olive oil
- Salt and pepper to taste

Instructions:

1. **Preheat Grill:** Preheat the grill to medium-high heat.
2. **Grill Corn:** Place the corn directly on the grill and cook for about 10-12 minutes, turning occasionally until charred.
3. **Cut Corn Off Cob:** Allow the corn to cool slightly, then cut the kernels off the cob.
4. **Mix Salad:** In a bowl, combine corn kernels, red bell pepper, red onion, jalapeño, lime juice, olive oil, salt, and pepper. Mix well.
5. **Serve:** Serve the salad warm or at room temperature.

Grilled Spinach and Feta Stuffed Portobellos

Ingredients:

- 4 large portobello mushrooms, stems removed
- 2 cups fresh spinach, chopped
- 1/2 cup feta cheese, crumbled
- 2 cloves garlic, minced
- 2 tbsp olive oil
- Salt and pepper to taste

Instructions:

1. **Preheat Grill:** Preheat the grill to medium heat.
2. **Sauté Spinach:** In a skillet, heat olive oil over medium heat. Add garlic and spinach, cooking until the spinach is wilted.
3. **Mix Filling:** In a bowl, combine sautéed spinach, feta cheese, salt, and pepper.
4. **Stuff Mushrooms:** Fill each portobello cap with the spinach and feta mixture.
5. **Grill Mushrooms:** Place the stuffed mushrooms on the grill and cook for about 5-7 minutes until the mushrooms are tender.
6. **Serve:** Serve warm as a delicious appetizer or side dish.

Enjoy your flavorful grilled dishes!

BBQ Sweet Potato Wedges

Ingredients:

- 2 large sweet potatoes, cut into wedges
- 2 tbsp olive oil
- 1 tbsp BBQ seasoning
- Salt and pepper to taste

Instructions:

1. **Preheat Grill:** Preheat the grill to medium-high heat.
2. **Prepare Sweet Potatoes:** In a bowl, toss sweet potato wedges with olive oil, BBQ seasoning, salt, and pepper.
3. **Grill Wedges:** Place the wedges on the grill, cooking for about 15-20 minutes, turning occasionally until tender and slightly charred.
4. **Serve:** Serve warm with your favorite dipping sauce.

Grilled Vegetable Fajitas

Ingredients:

- 1 bell pepper, sliced
- 1 onion, sliced
- 1 zucchini, sliced
- 1 tsp olive oil
- 1 tsp fajita seasoning
- Tortillas for serving

Instructions:

1. **Preheat Grill:** Preheat the grill to medium heat.
2. **Mix Vegetables:** In a bowl, toss the sliced vegetables with olive oil and fajita seasoning.
3. **Grill Vegetables:** Place the vegetables on the grill and cook for about 8-10 minutes, turning occasionally until tender and charred.
4. **Serve:** Serve the grilled vegetables in tortillas with your favorite toppings.

BBQ Vegetable Flatbreads

Ingredients:

- 4 flatbreads or naan
- 1 cup mixed vegetables (zucchini, bell peppers, onions)
- 1/2 cup BBQ sauce
- 1 cup shredded mozzarella cheese

Instructions:

1. **Preheat Grill:** Preheat the grill to medium heat.
2. **Grill Vegetables:** Toss mixed vegetables with olive oil and grill for about 5-7 minutes until tender.
3. **Assemble Flatbreads:** Spread BBQ sauce on each flatbread, top with grilled vegetables and cheese.
4. **Grill Flatbreads:** Place flatbreads on the grill for about 5 minutes until the cheese is melted and bubbly.
5. **Serve:** Slice and serve warm.

Grilled Garlic and Herb Zucchini

Ingredients:

- 2 zucchinis, sliced lengthwise
- 2 tbsp olive oil
- 2 cloves garlic, minced
- 1 tsp dried oregano
- Salt and pepper to taste

Instructions:

1. **Preheat Grill:** Preheat the grill to medium heat.
2. **Mix Marinade:** In a bowl, whisk together olive oil, garlic, oregano, salt, and pepper.
3. **Marinate Zucchini:** Brush the zucchini slices with the marinade.
4. **Grill Zucchini:** Grill the zucchini for about 5-7 minutes on each side until tender and grill marks appear.
5. **Serve:** Serve warm as a side dish.

BBQ Lentil and Quinoa Salad

Ingredients:

- 1 cup cooked lentils
- 1 cup cooked quinoa
- 1 bell pepper, diced
- 1/2 cup corn (fresh or frozen)
- 1/4 cup BBQ sauce
- Salt and pepper to taste

Instructions:

1. **Mix Ingredients:** In a bowl, combine cooked lentils, quinoa, bell pepper, corn, BBQ sauce, salt, and pepper.
2. **Chill Salad:** Refrigerate for at least 30 minutes to allow flavors to meld.
3. **Serve:** Serve chilled or at room temperature as a hearty salad.

Grilled Watermelon Salad

Ingredients:

- 4 slices of watermelon
- 1/4 cup feta cheese, crumbled
- Fresh mint leaves
- Balsamic glaze for drizzling

Instructions:

1. **Preheat Grill:** Preheat the grill to medium heat.
2. **Grill Watermelon:** Grill watermelon slices for about 2-3 minutes on each side until grill marks appear.
3. **Assemble Salad:** Arrange grilled watermelon on a plate, sprinkle with feta cheese and mint leaves.
4. **Drizzle:** Drizzle with balsamic glaze and serve immediately.

BBQ Mushroom and Black Bean Chili

Ingredients:

- 1 cup mushrooms, chopped
- 1 can (15 oz) black beans, drained and rinsed
- 1 cup diced tomatoes
- 1 onion, chopped
- 2 cloves garlic, minced
- 1 tbsp chili powder
- Salt and pepper to taste

Instructions:

1. **Sauté Ingredients:** In a pot, sauté onions and garlic until translucent. Add mushrooms and cook until softened.
2. **Add Remaining Ingredients:** Stir in black beans, diced tomatoes, chili powder, salt, and pepper.
3. **Simmer Chili:** Let simmer for about 20 minutes, stirring occasionally.
4. **Serve:** Serve warm, garnished with fresh herbs or avocado.

Grilled Stuffed Zucchini Boats

Ingredients:

- 4 medium zucchinis, halved and hollowed out
- 1 cup cooked rice or quinoa
- 1/2 cup marinara sauce
- 1/2 cup shredded cheese (optional)

Instructions:

1. **Preheat Grill:** Preheat the grill to medium heat.
2. **Mix Filling:** In a bowl, combine cooked rice or quinoa with marinara sauce.
3. **Stuff Zucchini:** Fill each zucchini half with the rice mixture and sprinkle with cheese if using.
4. **Grill Zucchini:** Place stuffed zucchinis on the grill and cook for about 10-12 minutes until tender.
5. **Serve:** Serve warm as a satisfying main dish.

Enjoy these delicious grilled recipes!

Smoky BBQ Pasta Salad

Ingredients:

- 8 oz pasta (your choice)
- 1 cup cherry tomatoes, halved
- 1 cup corn (fresh or frozen)
- 1/2 cup red onion, diced
- 1 cup black beans, drained and rinsed
- 1/2 cup BBQ sauce
- 1/4 cup olive oil
- Salt and pepper to taste

Instructions:

1. **Cook Pasta:** Cook pasta according to package instructions; drain and let cool.
2. **Mix Salad Ingredients:** In a large bowl, combine cooled pasta, cherry tomatoes, corn, red onion, and black beans.
3. **Prepare Dressing:** In a small bowl, whisk together BBQ sauce, olive oil, salt, and pepper.
4. **Combine:** Pour dressing over the pasta salad and toss to combine.
5. **Chill and Serve:** Refrigerate for at least 30 minutes before serving to allow flavors to meld.

Grilled Pita with Hummus and Vegetables

Ingredients:

- 4 pita bread
- 1 cup hummus (store-bought or homemade)
- 1 cucumber, sliced
- 1 bell pepper, sliced
- 1 cup cherry tomatoes, halved
- Olive oil for brushing
- Salt and pepper to taste

Instructions:

1. **Preheat Grill:** Preheat the grill to medium heat.
2. **Prepare Pita:** Brush pita bread with olive oil on both sides.
3. **Grill Pita:** Place pita on the grill and cook for about 2-3 minutes per side until warm and slightly crispy.
4. **Assemble:** Spread hummus on each pita and top with cucumber, bell pepper, and cherry tomatoes. Season with salt and pepper.
5. **Serve:** Cut into wedges and serve immediately.

BBQ Roasted Brussels Sprouts

Ingredients:

- 1 lb Brussels sprouts, trimmed and halved
- 2 tbsp olive oil
- 1/4 cup BBQ sauce
- Salt and pepper to taste

Instructions:

1. **Preheat Oven:** Preheat the oven to 400°F (200°C).
2. **Toss Brussels Sprouts:** In a bowl, toss Brussels sprouts with olive oil, BBQ sauce, salt, and pepper.
3. **Roast:** Spread Brussels sprouts on a baking sheet in a single layer and roast for 20-25 minutes, stirring halfway through, until tender and caramelized.
4. **Serve:** Serve warm as a side dish.

Grilled Radishes with Butter

Ingredients:

- 1 bunch radishes, trimmed
- 2 tbsp butter, melted
- Salt and pepper to taste
- Fresh herbs for garnish (optional)

Instructions:

1. **Preheat Grill:** Preheat the grill to medium heat.
2. **Prepare Radishes:** Toss radishes with melted butter, salt, and pepper.
3. **Grill Radishes:** Place radishes on the grill and cook for about 5-7 minutes, turning occasionally until tender and slightly charred.
4. **Serve:** Garnish with fresh herbs if desired and serve warm.

BBQ Jerk Tofu

Ingredients:

- 14 oz firm tofu, drained and pressed
- 2 tbsp jerk seasoning
- 2 tbsp olive oil
- 1/4 cup BBQ sauce

Instructions:

1. **Prepare Tofu:** Cut tofu into cubes or slabs.
2. **Marinate Tofu:** In a bowl, combine tofu with jerk seasoning, olive oil, and BBQ sauce; let marinate for at least 30 minutes.
3. **Preheat Grill:** Preheat the grill to medium-high heat.
4. **Grill Tofu:** Place tofu on the grill and cook for about 4-5 minutes per side until charred and heated through.
5. **Serve:** Serve with additional BBQ sauce on the side.

Enjoy these flavorful recipes!

Grilled Tomato and Mozzarella Salad

Ingredients:

- 2 cups cherry tomatoes, halved
- 8 oz fresh mozzarella, cubed
- 1/4 cup fresh basil leaves, torn
- 2 tbsp balsamic glaze
- 1 tbsp olive oil
- Salt and pepper to taste

Instructions:

1. **Preheat Grill:** Preheat the grill to medium heat.
2. **Grill Tomatoes:** Thread cherry tomatoes onto skewers and grill for about 2-3 minutes until slightly charred.
3. **Combine Ingredients:** In a large bowl, combine grilled tomatoes, mozzarella, and basil.
4. **Dress Salad:** Drizzle with balsamic glaze and olive oil; season with salt and pepper.
5. **Serve:** Toss gently and serve immediately.

BBQ Vegetable Stir-Fry

Ingredients:

- 1 zucchini, sliced
- 1 bell pepper, sliced
- 1 red onion, sliced
- 1 cup broccoli florets
- 2 tbsp soy sauce
- 2 tbsp BBQ sauce
- 1 tbsp olive oil
- Sesame seeds for garnish

Instructions:

1. **Preheat Grill or Wok:** Preheat grill or a wok on medium-high heat.
2. **Prepare Vegetables:** In a large bowl, toss all vegetables with olive oil, soy sauce, and BBQ sauce.
3. **Stir-Fry:** Cook vegetables in a grill basket or wok for 7-10 minutes, stirring frequently until tender.
4. **Garnish:** Sprinkle with sesame seeds before serving.

Grilled Citrus Marinated Tofu

Ingredients:

- 14 oz firm tofu, drained and pressed
- Juice of 1 orange
- Juice of 1 lime
- 2 tbsp soy sauce
- 1 tbsp olive oil
- 1 tsp garlic powder
- Salt and pepper to taste

Instructions:

1. **Marinate Tofu:** In a bowl, mix orange juice, lime juice, soy sauce, olive oil, garlic powder, salt, and pepper. Cut tofu into slabs and marinate for at least 30 minutes.
2. **Preheat Grill:** Preheat the grill to medium-high heat.
3. **Grill Tofu:** Grill tofu for 4-5 minutes on each side until charred and heated through.
4. **Serve:** Serve with grilled vegetables or salad.

BBQ Chickpea and Avocado Wraps

Ingredients:

- 1 can chickpeas, drained and rinsed
- 1 avocado, mashed
- 1 tbsp BBQ sauce
- 1/2 tsp cumin
- Salt and pepper to taste
- 4 whole wheat tortillas
- Fresh spinach or lettuce

Instructions:

1. **Mash Chickpeas:** In a bowl, mash chickpeas and mix with mashed avocado, BBQ sauce, cumin, salt, and pepper.
2. **Assemble Wraps:** Spread mixture onto tortillas, adding fresh spinach or lettuce.
3. **Wrap:** Roll up tortillas tightly and slice in half.
4. **Serve:** Serve immediately or wrap in foil for a picnic.

Grilled Fruit Skewers

Ingredients:

- 1 pineapple, peeled and cut into chunks
- 2 peaches, pitted and cut into wedges
- 1 cup strawberries, hulled
- 1 tbsp honey
- 1 tsp cinnamon (optional)

Instructions:

1. **Prepare Skewers:** Thread fruit onto skewers, alternating between pineapple, peaches, and strawberries.
2. **Brush with Honey:** Brush skewers lightly with honey and sprinkle with cinnamon if desired.
3. **Preheat Grill:** Preheat the grill to medium heat.
4. **Grill Fruit:** Grill fruit skewers for about 5-7 minutes, turning occasionally, until fruit is tender and caramelized.
5. **Serve:** Serve warm as a dessert or snack.

Enjoy these delicious recipes!